LIFE BEGINS

AT

SEVENTY-FIVE

A time of fulfillment and opportunity

NANCY ORLANDO

NANCY ORLANDO BOOKS

Cincinnati, Ohio

Nancyorlando-books.com

Printed in the United States of America

ISBN 978-0-9905599-3-1

Nancy Orlando Books

Cincinnati, Ohio

Nancyorlando-books.com

DEDICATION

Dedicated to every senior who thinks retirement is the end.... time to find a rocking chair and wait for the fat lady to sing!

We all had dreams that we didn't pursue for one reason or another. Take another look at them. If they still appeal to you, go for it! After all, you have time to write a book. You have time to paint a picture or find the right sunset to photograph? ....and don't worry about using some of that money you planned to leave to the kids. Use it wisely and enjoy it.

You have the time for dreams now. Once you get involved in whatever pleases or amuses you, you'll be amazed at how young and independent you feel. So don't think about it.........Do it. Just do it!

PREFACE

When I tell little stories about my life I always hear comments like — "Why don't you write a book?" Or "You could write a great book."

I decided I would write a memoir about how my life took on a totally new direction when most people are winding down into a cozy retirement. "Life Begins at Seventy Five" would be a light humorous story of my memories. I began to write and before the second page was completed I realized my life had not been a bit funny. Through the years I had laughed a lot, but seeing the words on paper, I wondered why! Now I wonder how I will describe my book. I guess the only thing to do is ramble on, tell my story and see where it goes.

Table of Contents

Life begins AT SEVENTY FIVE!

Chapter One

That Magic Year

I know. You think I've had a "senior moment" and forgotten that magic age when "life begins". I know the old wives tale you are thinking of. I remember my 40th birthday very clearly. All I could think about was "life begins at 40". If there was any truth to it, I couldn't wait for it to begin.

My life at that point had been difficult, to say the least. A "too young" marriage had resulted in four children and 13 years of humiliation and heart break. There was enough darkness

and ugliness to fill a book on

just those years. Some stories,

however, are better not shared. Let it

suffice to say I was relieved when he

left us. It's far better to be lonely

by yourself than to be lonely with

someone.

     A year later I married a blind jazz

pianist. Bill filled my life and the

lives of my children with love,

laughter, pride and happiness. This

small man with his obvious limitations

possessed an endless supply of love and

wisdom. He gave of it generously. My

children gave him the title and eternal

love a child gives "daddy". To this day, "Daddy" means Bill.

He became my life coach. He awakened that little girl in me who had such big dreams. A long suppressed ego began to emerge. I discovered strengths and traits I would have sworn I did not have. My parents were concerned that I was marrying a blind man, someone I would have to guide through life. They soon learned, Bill was not blind - he just couldn't see. There is a vast difference. He was the most, well-adjusted human being I have ever known.

Everyone could see how much he loved me and I basked in that love. The comfort of finally knowing I had no rivals, gave me the freedom to be myself. There was barely enough money for the necessities of life, but that was all right. We had one another, his two children and my four. We adored them all. Life was challenging but filled with the love that makes life worthwhile.

I had always wanted to be a professional singer. Several years before we were married, I heard Bill playing at a hotel dining room. He played so beautifully I asked to sing with him. His agent was in the room and asked me to sing on his television show. I did several guest spots on his show and he booked some benefit jobs for me with his band. I also sang with Bill on some of his bookings.

Dressing the part of a professional singer was such an ego boost for me. I had no money for clothes but fortunately I was a capable seamstress. I went to the high end boutiques and tried on gorgeous dresses and gowns suitable for nightclub or supper club wear. In the dressing room I turned the dresses wrong side out to see how they were made. I

bought elegant fabrics and made clothes
that looked like the boutique gowns.

Bill was an original. He refused
to let his blindness hamper him from
doing anything. We had a very good
friend who had a twin engine Cessna
plane. He invited us for a short
Saturday afternoon ride. Bill was
seated in the co-pilot seat and I was in
the seat behind him. We flew around for
a few minutes looking at the south
Florida landscape and the bay of Naples.
Henry, our friend, said, "Take over
Bill." Bill said "What's this?" as he
pulled back on the stick in front of

him. The plane soared straight up until Henry leveled it out with his controls.

I couldn't see what Bill was doing but the plane dipped sharply to the right, then sharply to the left. Then it headed downward. Henry let Bill try everything before telling him to sit back for a landing. Bill was totally thrilled with his new accomplishment.

That night we arrived for work at the lounge in the Holiday Inn. The manager and his wife were there setting up new glasses they had purchased that afternoon. His wife asked me if we saw the drunk flying a plane that afternoon.

They saw him on the trip back from Miami. I asked her if the plane went straight up.

"Yes", she said.

"And did it dip from side to side? " I asked.

"Yes", she said excitedly. "You saw it too!"

"I was in it! I replied. "Guess who the pilot was?" Everyone knew Bill never touched alcohol after his heart attack years earlier. I pointed at Bill, who was sitting smugly at the piano, totally enjoying his new found notoriety.

Laughter was the norm in our home. Even when discipline was in order. Sometimes Bill would tell the boys to do something which they ignored. He would get up and stand just inches from a wall. He'd say, "Now wall, I want to have this conversation with you. Can you hear me wall?" The boys usually felt embarrassed and promptly did what was requested.

We laughed when we overheard my teen daughter on the phone say, "He's pretty cool for an old cat."

Six short years later, the August after my 39th birthday, I sat in his hospital room and watched this beautiful man sit up in his hospital bed. It was a movement that was physically impossible for his cancer ravaged body. He stretched his hand toward an unseen hand. His voice was filled with wonder and awe as he said "Oh, I'm going! I'm going". The smile on his face told me his blind eyes saw and his hand touched something so glorious, he could leave me without a look back. He fell back on his pillow, gone from me forever.

Yes, it would be nice if life would begin at 40. I was ready. Life did not begin. Each lonely day brought a new problem or challenge I was totally unprepared to deal with. By then my oldest daughter was married. That left only three to feed, clothe, worry and pray over. Three who had never received a penny in support from their father - not even so much as a card for a birthday or Christmas. How does a depressed lonely mother make up for that?

That year, my uncle, who was not in the habit of sending gifts, sent me a check for Christmas. It was enough to buy an inexpensive pool table. My two boys could bring their friends home to play pool. It kept the boys off the street and gave me a little peace of mind.

LIFE BEGINS AT SEVENTY FIVE!

Chapter two

Try Again

I was alone for almost three years, when I married again. A friend, who owned a neighborhood bar that Bill had played in, introduced me to him. She thought we both needed someone to take care of. There was no real courtship. We both needed someone and each was willing to help the other. He was my much needed friend every day.

In a few months, we set up an appointment with a justice of the peace in Newport to marry us. He had married

a couple at the Beverly Hills Supper
Club and had to come home for our
appointment. He had definitely had too
much to drink. We exchanged our vows and
drove home. We turned on the TV to hear
the news and discovered the Beverly
Hills Supper Club was on fire. Les told
me he wanted to go to hear John Davidson
at Beverly Hills but didn't think I
would want to take my daughter there, so
he didn't say anything. My sixteen year
old daughter had been my witness for the
wedding.

The next day we received a call
from the Justice of the Peace who had
married us. He thanked us for making

the appointment that made him leave the club. He said he knew he had too much to drink and would have had trouble escaping the fire. It became the only light thing about that night. Any time Les and I had a fuss, he would say "It's not legal....the preacher was drunk!"

Les was a good but troubled man. He owned a struggling paint and decorating business. The store had been at the right place at the right time and flourished for a number of years. When the building and restoration boom of the developing suburb ended, the store floundered. Instead of diversifying, or taking the business in a new direction, he sat alone, day after day, raving about the customers who were going to the big chain stores that had moved into the area. He knew the days of small retail businesses were over but he refused to close the store. A failing business, countless cigarettes and too many beers, turned this pleasant affable soul into a miserable, unhappy, negative man. When the IRS seized the store for unpaid taxes, he became suicidal.

Somehow Les managed to apply for jobs and was employed to match colors for after-market touch up paints. One evening, he stayed at the table after dinner, saying he would join me in the living room in a few minutes. I heard a

thud and ran to the dining room to find

him on the floor trying to crawl to the

bathroom. He said the pain in his groin

was so severe he couldn't stand up, but

insisted that I should not call 911. I

helped him to his feet and to the car in

the driveway.

At the Emergency Room, the doctor

said Les had a ruptured appendix. He

was given massive doses of antibiotics.

The infection had to be controlled

before he could be taken into surgery.

Several hours later he was rushed into

the operating room. After the surgery,

the doctor explained that because

peritonitis had set in, he had to remove

the intestines and organs from the lower abdomen. The cavity was flushed out and everything was washed before returning it to his body. He felt the surgery had been in time. They would continue the massive doses of antibiotics for several days and watch him closely. It had been a close call but Les would live.

After the surgery, he continued to have constant pain. He was unable to walk or move in a normal fashion. He supported his lower abdomen with his right hand to relieve the pain enough to walk. Returning to work was not an option. Numerous tests were run but no explanation for the pain was found. Our family doctor felt, as I did, that something was not properly replaced the night of the surgery, but nothing showed up on the MRI.

We applied for disability which was denied. My income was not enough to cover all our expenses. I had to sell my home for what I owed to avoid foreclosure. This left us with only my income, no funds to move on with and a fight to reverse the disability denial.

My father bought a tiny house in Kentucky which we could live in and make the mortgage payments. We thought life would finally be easier.

LIFE BEGINS AT SEVENTY FIVE

Chapter Three

Try TO GIVE BACK

It was eighteen months after the surgery before Lester's disability claim was finally awarded with the help of a lawyer. We tried to settle into life in the tiny house. With the settlement check for the months of waiting for the disability approval, he was able to buy a small yard barn. It was just big enough to keep a new yard tractor and other equipment that would allow him to do what he loved best - keep a beautiful yard.

The little house was close to my parent's home. Looking out for them became more and more difficult. Daddy had always been a very demanding man. He felt the help he had given us gave him total control over our lives. Les mowed his lawn and took him to bowling twice a week. He was expected to be available on call to take Daddy any where he wanted to go at any time. I was expected to stop at a grocery store after work nearly every night. Sometimes I had to stop at two stores to get the advertised specials. His health deteriorated along with his mental abilities. Each day he became more difficult.

One evening when I brought the groceries he wanted to the house, Daddy was in his recliner in the living room. Mother was busily trying to temp him into eating the beef stew she had made for him. It was one of his favorite meals, but he insisted she didn't make it the same as she always did. Mother had a spoon filled with stew trying to get him to taste it. He flung his arm out and nearly hit her. I knew they could no longer get along on their own. Mother had neither the physical strength nor the mental acumen to deal with his outbursts. He needed special care. Getting him into a nursing home would be a real challenge. As a little girl I had promised them they would never go to a nursing home. It was a promise I was reminded of, frequently, through the years.

Over the next few days, his temper grew worse and his motor skills deteriorated. Then he went into a coma. He had suffered with severe bursitis in his shoulder for years. We discovered he ran from doctor to doctor trying to get help. They would prescribe medication for arthritis. Daddy didn't tell them he was seeing several doctors for the same complaint and he took all the medicines they prescribed. The result was a destroyed pancreas and a diabetic coma.

The doctor at the hospital described the next terrifying days as a brain seizure. Daddy had to be restrained. He would throw anything he could reach. He screamed and raved and became a total mad man. He refused to eat, swearing we were trying to poison him. It took several days to bring his blood sugar under control so he could take therapy to restore his motor skills. A nursing home was the only possibility for us. I convinced him it would be a temporary thing. When he was stronger and calmer, we would take him home.

The nursing home near my parent's home was full but we found a very nice home a 30 minute drive away. When we took him from the hospital he required "skilled care" so the cost of the skilled nursing floor was covered by Medicare. We knew that need would probably end soon and he would go into the regular population at the regular and very expensive rate. There was a savings account that would cover things for a few months. Mother and I signed the papers agreeing to the financial responsibility. There was nothing else we could do but pray that he would recover enough to be able to live at home again.

At first, I picked Mother up after work and we went to see Daddy every night. We would get him ready for bed and stop on the way home to get something to eat. If he was still in the dining room when we arrived, we watched him eat. He sat at a table with two other patients and an aide. She tried to see that they all ate. Two of the patients were totally unable to feed themselves. The aide fed them. Daddy could load up the spoon with food. The aide was too busy feeding the others to see that his spoon was empty by the time it got to his mouth. I started feeding him his evening meal in his room. That way we were sure he had at least one good meal each day.

It wasn't long before I could see the toll it was taking on Mother. She could not keep up this pace. I might lose her first. I told her I would bring her on Wednesday and the weekends. I would go the other nights. Every night I would go into his room with the aide bringing his evening tray and say "Hi Daddy." He would lower his brow, stretch out his arm to point at me and say accusingly, "There's the reason I'm here." That really hurt but there was no other way to care for him.

One evening he was unusually restless and didn't look well at all. The Doctor was making rounds so I stayed to talk to him. The doctor checked Daddy and rang for the nurse. "Why wasn't I called?" he asked.

"We were watching and would have called if he didn't improved by tonight," was her response.

Daddy was immediately moved back to skilled care. The next day he went into a coma from which he never awoke.

Mother got through all the planning and the funeral far better than I thought she would. I continued to stop every night after work to see how she was. Daddy had been such a strong and domineering part of her life, I wanted her to experience a little independence.

After a few months she seemed less healthy and not as alert as she had been. She had enjoyed Kuchen, a miniature long haired dachshund for 17 years. It had been over a year since Kuchen had to be put down but she still talked about him often. I thought a dog might be some comfort to her. We found a two year old little dachshund needing

a home. She tried for two weeks but
just didn't have the energy to walk and
care for him. I knew her days of living
alone were over. We decided we would
sell both houses and build everyone's
house.

LIFE BEGINS AT SEVENTY FIVE!

Chapter Four

EVERYONE'S HOUSE

Everyone's house was a large ranch on two acres in a small rural community. We put Mother in the master bedroom where she had her own bath and a nice sitting area. She also had a walk in closet and that was the happiest part of the arrangement for her.

I had the movers leave all the boxes in the garage so we could keep the house from being too cluttered.

Mother stood admiring her closet. "This is mine?" she asked with a little girl look of joy on her face. I laughed because I knew why she was so happy.

My parents were both in the garment industry. Daddy was a presser and Mother was a power sewing machine operator and a hand finisher. They worked in men's clothing and Daddy was quite a dresser. He never went in public looking untidy. He even wore a suit and tie to the grocery store.

This meant he had a lot of clothes and accessories. He would commandeer every closet leaving very little space for Mother's clothes. He finally built a large wardrobe in the guest room on the second floor for her clothes. She happily ran up and down the steps to get to her closet. Now she looked at this eight by ten foot space like she was exploring a grand ballroom!

"It's all yours, Mama," I told her. "It's just for you!"

She smiled and studied the space for a moment. "Do you think that small chest of drawers would fit in the end there? I could keep my sweaters and underwear in that."

"I'm sure it will," I answered.

The chest was sitting in the bedroom across the hall. It was not a heavy piece of furniture so I pushed it into the back of the closet for her. She refused to let us bring the boxes with her things to the bedroom. She spent the rest of the day running back and forth to the garage, retrieving armloads of her things to put in her closet. By the end of the day, the little chest of drawers was filled and her jewelry boxes were carefully arranged on the top. The overhead shelves were filled and long rods on

each side were color coded with all her
clothes.

I soon discovered all was not going
well in "everyone's house." Mother had
really fallen for the dozens of letters
she received telling her of contests
that would make her rich.

Those scammers are experts at
convincing the elderly that they are
just one small check away from more
money that they have ever seen.

One day Les noticed Mother's bank
statement was a heavy packet. It was
obvious she had written a lot of checks.

She refused to talk about it or show me her statement. Daddy had arranged for the bank to hold a power of attorney to care for them if I ever needed it. I went to the bank and told them she was obviously writing a lot of checks. The banker brought her account up on line. That month she had sent $970 to those scammers in small checks anywhere from $7 to $20. She had an adequate income, but there was no way she could afford to continue to throw amounts like that away.

I talked to a lawyer about being named Mother's Guardian. I found that part of the process was a verbal examination in the court room. Mother would never have understood that and would have been totally humiliated. I could not put her through that.

The banker suggested I use the Power of Attorney Daddy had left for me and take over her account. He added my name to the account, showing it was for her care. I would have to sign any checks she wanted to write. This, of course, created many scenes. She would want to send a check to get the money she was sure she had won. Pointing out the small print telling her she had not won anything was useless. She didn't believe me.

The only thing I could do was get to
our rural mail box before she did and
throw away all the contest mail. I
heard our local state representative was
writing a bill to stop some of the
misery those scam artists were causing
Kentucky Seniors. I called her and
offered to help in any way I could. I
went to Frankfort to testify about the
money Mother was throwing away each
month. My foggy morning trip was really
a waste of time. The lobbyists for the
scammers were everywhere. I have never
come so close to being physically
violent as I was that day.

The bill being considered was a requirement controlling the size of the lettering in the mailings. We wanted the fact that you had not won, to be stated in letters as large as the lead line, so carefully worded to make the recipient sure they had already won. The lobbyists wanted the requirement reduced to a smaller font.

A female representative of one of the scam companies had a paper showing the font they would agree to. I said, "My Mother cannot read that small print. At 86 she only reads large heavy print." That horrible woman looked at me and said in her most condescending tone,

"That's your mother's problem." That is
the only time in my life I have been
angry enough to want to harm someone.
It took every bit of strength I could
muster to keep my hands off that
horrible woman's neck!

The lobbyists won and a watered
down useless version of the bill was
passed. I received a beautiful citation
from the State House of Representatives
and became an honorary Kentucky Colonel
for my efforts to help protect the
seniors of Kentucky. That was very nice
but I would much rather have seen the
bill passed with some teeth in it, to
limit the success of those scammers.

The representative said she would try again in the next session. Caring for Mother and meeting all the challenges awaiting me, made it impossible for me to continue to help or know the outcome of her efforts.

LIFE BEGINS AT SEVENTY FIVE!

Chapter Five

Not Again!

In 1999, we were barely settled in the house when Les developed a severe shaking in his left hand. I told him it was probably Parkinson's and could be treated with medication. He finally agreed to go to the doctor.

The doctor did a regular work up and took chest x-rays. A large mass was discovered and Les was sent to a specialist. She diagnosed advanced lung cancer. I knew that's what it was but having already lost a man I loved to this horrible disease, when I heard the word, I burst into tears. Les put his hand on mine and said, "You sure can pick 'em, can't you honey." The man had just received a death sentence and he felt sorry for me!

Hospice provided a hospital bed which we put in the family room. It was a bright room where Les could see the fountain in the little pond we had built and the hummingbird feeder by the pond. The room was big enough, I had a roll away bed at the foot of his bed so I could hear him during the night if he needed care.

Mother stayed in her room most of the time. Her eyesight was so poor she was legally blind. I ordered talking books for her, which she loved. Her health was fairly good but mentally she was deteriorating rapidly.

Retirement was out of the question when I turned 65 that year. I knew I would be alone again and would need all the income I could get to care for Mother and try to keep the house. Fortunately I loved my job as a specialist in the county housing program, so I continued to work.

For most people, sixty five is the
time you get a pat on the back or a kick
in the pants for your financial planning
or lack thereof. For me, it simply
added a lot of junk mail to my mailbox.
Apparently, it is universally agreed
that certain infirmities occur on your
sixty fifth birthday. Every hearing aid
company, eyeglass doctor, power chair
vender and step-in-tub manufacturer sent
me their sales pitch along with their
birthday greetings.

We managed without help. Lester
could phone me if Mother needed help.
He was able to manage for himself for a
short time. My daughter, Mary Ellen and

a volunteer with the Cancer Society saw to it that he went for his treatments.

I was concerned about Lester. I wasn't sure he understood that his life was nearly over. He had never expressed any interest in my religion but he did talk about camp meetings when he was a little boy. I talked to the minister at the local Baptist Church and he agreed to visit Lester to see if he wanted to talk. Les told him he enjoyed the music at those camp meetings.

The minister brought a quartet from the church to sing gospel music for him. Les really enjoyed the music and the

group was so kind to him. Snowball, a
white cat, Les had taken in several
years earlier, sat at the foot of his
bed while the quartet sang. At the end
of one hymn you could hear Snowball's
loud meows chiming in with the voices.
The tenor said, "That's the note I've
been trying to find!"

In September, Lester's last night
was an agonizing struggle for him
because of the inefficiency of the local
Hospice Group. Somehow, the morphine
that would ease his pain and relax him
so he could simply go to sleep was not
ordered. By the time the error was
corrected and the medication arrived, he

was in such pain and misery it was an
unbearable sight for his family gathered
around him. It is a terrifying memory
that time can never erase. We are all
very sure he is in heaven. We watched
him travel through hell to get there.

LIFE BEGINS AT SEVENTY FIVE

Chapter Six

Mama

With Lester gone, I had to hire someone to keep an eye on Mother while I worked. We found a woman who was willing to stay with her for the small amount I could afford to pay her. She spoiled Mother and Mother enjoyed the attention.

By now her mind was more confused than ever. Early in her mental problems, she knew her brain wasn't working right. She would slap herself on her temples and say, "My brain doesn't work right." Many times she would go to her room and cry. I can remember praying she would get so bad she didn't know something was wrong.

I think she had finally reached that point. I am an only child but she would ask me, "Are you the one who is here in the morning or are you the one who comes at night?" On one hospital stay she told the nurse she had two daughters.

The one person she never forgot was her mother. She died just before Mother's first day of school in 1919. The oval picture of her was always in a

prominent place in Mother's home. I
hung it at the end of the hall in
"everyone's house". The door to the
mother's master bedroom was on the
right. Anytime Mother walked down that
hall her eyes were on that picture.
Sometimes I thought she spoke to it as
she went into her room.

I knew what a horrible childhood
Mama had with a step mother who was
jealous of her. She was too small to
remember her mother's touch or her
voice. Mama and I were so close, I
couldn't imagine spending your entire
life without the love and closeness of
your mother.

We had installed a small pond at the edge of the back brick patio. It had a fountain in the center and a big fish figure at one end that spewed water from it mouth, back into the pond. A glider with a shade roof over it sat at the end of the pond. I would take Mother there to sit on the glider and listen to the water splashing into the pond several times a day. There were three gold fish in the pond. We named them Larry, Curly and Moe. They had grown so big I had to put up a no fishing sign to stop the threats from the grandchildren to fish in Grandma's pond.

Mother turned 86 in May of that year. We decided to have a family get together and have a birthday party for her. A beautiful full sheet cake was ordered and we decided we would put all 86 candles on the cake. It took several of us to get them all installed and lit. When the great grandchildren blew them out for her, everyone was shocked when a huge cloud of smoke filled the dining room. Someone picked up the cake and ran for the front door to clear the smoke. We told Mother if we did that next year we would have to get a burn permit from the fire department!

With Mother's income and my Social Security, we got along well enough that I was able to cut my work to three days a week. That gave me more time to spend with Mother.

One day my daughter-in-law was covering for Mother's companion who needed the day off. I looked in on mother before leaving for work. She was stretched out on the bed, covered with vomit. We did our best to prop her up and tried to clean her up but it was obvious she had aspirated and needed help immediately. We called 911 and she was rushed to the local hospital. I always took her to the hospital just across the river in Ohio when I was able to take her in the car. The ambulance had to take her to the closest hospital. In the Emergency Room I asked to have her transported to the other hospital. The doctor told me she was so ill she probably would not live through that transfer. I told them to call a priest and admit her.

Mother had been ready to leave this life for a long time. In spite of numerous near death trips to the hospital, she survived. Every time I brought her home, she was furious because she wasn't dead yet.

This appeared to be the time she
was waiting for. The expression on her
face, when she realized the priest was
administering last rites, is something I
will never forget. She was so at peace
and more content than I had ever seen
her. I couldn't help but pray that we
all could be that prepared when our time
comes.

They put her in a bed with rails
all around it like a big crib. Mother
had such tiny veins it was hard to put a
needle in her to take blood. It was a
painful horrible experience for her.
The next morning, several nurses came in
to take blood. My frail, near deaths

door, Mother, jumped to her feet in her bed with her fists in the air, screaming "No blood! No Way! No How!" I laughed and called the relatives in Cleveland to tell them she was going to come away from deaths door one more time. In one of our short conversations that day, she reminded me that I would have a lot of money now, if I had let her send those checks in to win the contests.

That night I had to call relatives again. Mama would not be angry again. She was finally where she wanted to be. I prayed that God sent her mother to hold her and show her around.

LIFE BEGINS AT SEVENTY FIVE

Chapter seven

Alone again

Everyone's house had been built
with three incomes to support it. With
Les and Mother gone, there was only one
income to make all the payments. I had
also run up credit card debt to make
things comfortable for everyone in the
new house. It was very difficult to
make ends meet with just my income.
Common sense told me I should sell the
house but I persevered. I had a home I
was really proud of. Inside, it was
finished very economically but I thought
I could add the nice touches over the

years. I struggled each month to keep my world from tumbling down. I was so grateful I had managed to keep the house while Mother was alive. She could not have gone through another move.

With no one to take care of, I had time for new things. I decided to try to write. From the time I was a very little girl I wanted to be a writer. In high school I decided I should write about growing up during World War Two. I told my favorite English teacher about it. She said it was a great idea and I should write the book. I told her I would write it when I grew up.

Maybe now was the time for writing. I had a computer my son had built for me. Internet service was very poor and the computer was very slow which made any research nearly impossible. I slowly tried to put words on paper but was never satisfied with what I had written.

Life can be so cruel. Losing Les and losing Mother were just the first heartaches. My grandson, Carl, had just gotten out of the marines and married his California sweetheart. They had just bought a house when he was diagnosed with brain cancer. They tried to tell me he was getting better and there was hope. Then, they had to say if I wanted to see him alive I should come right now. He was my first grandchild. I said I never understood eternity until I held him in my arms. He was my step into eternity and now that step was taken away.

Somehow time marched on. I enjoyed my work as a housing specialist with the county HUD housing program. I considered a second job but 40 hours, two acres and a seven room home left little energy for another job. Somehow 2002 and 2003 slipped by. Every month was a financial struggle trying to keep the house. It was painfully obvious, the house must be sold.

In earlier years I had sent a Christmas Letter instead of cards. I always typed them and mailed Xerox copies. I hadn't sent cards or letters at Christmas for a number of years. Now I had the computer to make it easier to write and print my letters. I decided I would go back to sending a letter to everyone.

MERRY CHRISTMAS!   HAPPY NEW YEAR!

Once again, "'Tis the season." I will
certainly not be sad to bid goodbye to
2004.

As most of you know, my beloved
grandson, Carl, lost his battle with
brain cancer, January 7. It has been a
devastating loss for our entire family.

In July, my grandson Brandon, a
marine, was sent to Iraq. He is
stationed near Baghdad. It's such a
horrible fearful war and all we can do
is watch the daily news and pray.

All this along with planning to put
the house on the market left me with no
will to even fake some Christmas spirit
- until today.

When Lester was a little boy a
neighbor lady gave him an old-fashioned
amaryllis plant. His Mother cared for
it throughout her life. As "Lester's
Lilly" multiplied she gave a new plant
to everyone in the family. It blooms
twice a year. Since Lester's death, the
plant she passed on to me, has bloomed
every Christmas. I always feel my gift
from Lester has arrived when it blooms.

I walked into the family room this morning and discovered my Christmas present had arrived early. The amaryllis is loaded with buds and two stems filled with beautiful orange blooms greeted me. That was the push I needed.

All my decorations are stored anticipating the sale of the house. I only have the aluminum tree I was going to sell. I put it up and wove ribbons through it to match my living room. It's not my traditional tree filled with memories, but it will do. All my local family will be with me. I know they will turn this messed up season into another precious memory. We have a new little person too. Terry, great grandbaby number 11 arrived in October.

In spite of being a little blue, I know I am the luckiest old lady alive. I'm spry and healthy enough to keep working at seventy. I have a wonderful family to love and be loved by. Not only that – How many people do you know who get flowers from heaven for Christmas?

Love and God bless each one of you,

Nancy

LIFE BEGINS AT SEVENTY FIVE

Chapter Eight

The final Blow

I have always been a pet person. A house without a cat and/or a dog just can't be a home.

With Lester gone, I had to deal with Beau, a feisty little dog Lester had adopted several years before. He had been in two abusive homes and retaliated to anything he thought was a threat with snarls and attempts to bite. We thought a loving home would correct his behavior but it did not. Not too long after Les was gone, Beau developed

a cough. The vet discovered cancer.
His lungs were peppered with the
disease. With his disposition it was
impossible to take care of him. It broke
my heart but I decided to put him to
sleep.

I pray pets get to join owners in
heaven. I held Beau while he went to
sleep for the last time and told him to
find Lester. I know Lester loved him
and I think Beau was learning to trust
Les. I like to think of the two of
them, together, in that wonderful place.

George Bush started his second term
as president with high expectations for

all his proposals. I cringed at his idea to privatize Social Security. I received my first husband's amount which was several hundred dollars higher than any of the others. I was fearful I would get a smaller check if Social Security was changed.

Then the new federal budgets were announced. The county housing program was severely cut and expenses would have to be trimmed. Being well past retirement age and working part time, it was only logical that my position could be eliminated. That was a blow I hadn't considered. When you take someone's job, his or her world falls apart. I

applied for my unemployment and started
searching for work. I was determined to
keep the house.

I didn't have the computer skills
for the good office jobs. I found
myself competing with the young workers
for the low skilled and low paid service
and manufacturing starter jobs.

I spent days at the unemployment
office searching the jobs screens and
applying for interviews. Money became
even more critical. My dream house in
the country added distance and travel
cost to applying for work. The

unemployment check barely bought gas and a few groceries.

I couldn't be selective, I took any jobs I was offered. I thought being a cashier at the big chain grocery store would be a good job. I was hired but not for the job I wanted. They put me in the delicatessen. At four foot nine inches high I had problems reaching things and seeing over the high refrigerated counters. The other workers were all the age of my children and grandchildren. I guess they were curious about the white haired old lady and we got along very well.

One evening a little old lady about my size came in. She was asking questions about the various lunch meats in the case. I stood on my tip toes trying to see her and answer her. One of the young men came over and lifted me in the air by my waist so I could talk to my customer! It was a fun job but I can't say I was a successful deli worker.

I finally was moved to cashier. The computerized registers were a challenge but the biggest problem was the hours. I needed full time work but was never assigned 40 hours. Usually I worked under 30 hours. At the hourly rate my money problems got worse. I got a job at another super market that promised more hours. I found that retail businesses are notorious for not keeping promises. I moved on to another job doing phone surveys. If you want to feel totally despised, conduct a few surveys. You keep telling people, "only a few more questions" until they finally deliver a few choice words and hang up on you.

I finally had to admit defeat. The house was put on the market. I soon discovered my dream home wasn't' worth as much as I thought it should be, plus it didn't seem to be anyone else's dream home. Showings were scarce and hopes for a sale were dim. The price was reduced and a few showings produced some interest. Finally an offer came in.

I probably would have turned it down if my financial situation wasn't so critical. I signed the sale and arranged for the repairs and changes required in the contract. Now I had a new problem. I had no idea where I would go or what I would call home.

My daughter, Mary Ellen, and son-in-law, Jeffery lived just a mile or two away. They were living in a double wide while they restored a 200 year old log cabin. It was a labor of love they had worked on for several years. They asked me to move in with them. I could help them a bit with finances while they got the cabin ready to move into. Then I would take over the double wide. It made perfect sense and gave me a future to plan for. They lived on a ridge with beautiful views of the surrounding valley and distant hills. I loved the place and living next to my daughter was appealing too.

Preparing to move was a nightmare. I sold anything I could do without. Everything else was packed. Jeff built a building that would eventually become his workshop. Furniture I wanted to keep and the boxes were stored there.

They emptied the two small bedrooms for me. I put the bedroom set my parents bought when Daddy's mother discovered Mama was pregnant, in one room. Grandma was visiting the furnished apartment they lived in. She scolded Daddy severely because he didn't even own the bed he made a baby in! That story has turned that inexpensive veneer four poster bedroom set into a precious family heirloom. The other room became my den for the computer, my books and things I wanted to keep out of storage.

It took time to get settled in but it worked well. It took a bit longer for the pets to adjust. I had adopted a 16 pound-mostly shitzu - pound puppy at our local shelter. He was the perfect companion for me with one exception. He insisted on chasing my cat. Snowball had become a bit of a hermit after his arrival. Now we had a double problem. Mary Ellen had a cat too.

Poor Gizmo went through a lot of "time-outs" for scaring one cat or the other. It took time but he learned the cats were off limits.

I took over the grocery shopping and cooking. It kept me busy but left time for writing. I was determined but I just couldn't get the words I wanted on paper.

My Christmas letter that year was a real challenge.........I tried not to sound as depressed as I was. I talked about the jobs I tried to do. I had often joked and said "if it isn't immoral or illegal, I have probably done it at least once". I told everyone I found lots of jobs I had never done before.

I wrote about the job that reminded me of Lucille Ball in the candy factory. I worked in a print shop in front of a machine that folded big sheets of medical information down to the size of a business card. They popped out about four times faster than I could pack them into narrow little boxes to ship. When I couldn't keep up they just kept popping out and piled up on the floor around me. Not easy to keep the boss from knowing I'd screwed up again! For another one, I drove around a gigantic warehouse on a little cart, pulling auto repair hoses and belts for shipment. I finally had to admit, it was fun but I wasn't strong enough or fast enough for factory jobs and the pay was too low for me to keep the house anyway. I finally had to give up and sell the house. It's been hard but it's nice at 71, to not go to work every day and not worry about finding enough money to scrape through another month.

Living with Mary Ellen and Jeff has worked out just fine. Moving a second family into space that's perfect for one has turned our space into a sardine can. Fortunately we all have a good sense of humor. We laugh a lot and eat well. I've gained 15 pounds. That's what laughter and food will do for you - now I need to diet!

By next Christmas the kids should be in the log cabin. Next Christmas will be my year. When I get my things out of storage they will seem new. What a great way to start over!

LIFE BEGINS AT SEVENTY FIVE

Chapter Nine

Life on the Ridge

I really loved living in the country. Gizmo, my Shitzu pet loved it too. We walked the long drive to the log cabin at the back of the hay field every day. My son-in-law's sister in Florida owned it. It had a covered porch clear across the front. She had furnished the porch with a swing, chairs and tables made of willow. She made a few of the pieces herself. Sitting on that porch was like visiting another time and another place.

I fed the birds but had to fight
with the raccoons to see that the birds
got the food. I kept a box of rocks on
the porch and called them my "coon
rocks". When a raccoon tried to get
into a bird feeder I threw rocks at it.
They quickly learned the maximum
distance I could throw so they could
stand just out of reach at the edge of
the hill and stare at me. They looked
so sweet and innocent it was really
laughable. Mary Ellen was sure they
would throw the rocks back soon.

They are such intelligent, devious
little creatures. I kept a plastic bin,
filled with sunflower seeds under the

bench on the porch. One day, the bin
was missing. I discovered the raccoons
had decided to take it home. They
pushed it across the porch, down the
steps, and across the yard to the edge
of the hill. It was about half way down
the hill, caught on a fallen tree. The
top was scraped and shredded where they
had tried to chew into it. If it hadn't
been for the tree I probably would never
have found it.

When I wasn't' enjoying the scenery
and the critters, I really worked on my
book. I read everything I could find on
writing memoir. Then I found the book
Storycatcher by Christina Baldwin. I

was sure if I could spend some time with this woman she could help me get my book on paper. I discovered that she held seminars. It would be expensive but I really felt it was something I needed to do.

What a wonderful experience it was! Walking through the marsh every morning to Marsh House where we met each day, was exhilarating. We sat on the floor in a big circle. The group was such a wonderful mix of personalities, skills and life stories. After the first session I felt connected to each and every one of them.

The accommodations were as eclectic as the participants. I had the best room. Most of the group were housed two to a room. I think because of the age difference, I was assigned a room by myself. I was old enough to be the mother of most or the grandmother of a few. My room was large with a wall of windows looking out on the garden and the woods beyond. I couldn't ask for a more beautiful place to find the inspiration to write.

Christina spent some personal time with each one of us. She talked about my book, read what I had written and helped me determine the point of beginning for my story. I was finally able to start putting it on paper.

I was amazed at how quickly we became a cohesive community. Mid week we had one full day of silence. Not a word was spoken. Even our meals were taken in silence. That day was so productive! I sat at my desk and the words just poured out. By the time I headed home I had managed to get the basics of my book down. I was clear on where I was headed and what I needed to write. After all the years of confusion, it was such a relief. It was an experience I will always cherish. Every moment is etched in my memory.

When I returned home I spent all my free time in my den. Pumpkin sat at my feet and Snowball curled up on the window sill. I had much to write about for Christmas that year. Time really does heal if we let it. I was actually doing things I could only dream of doing before. I wasn't ready to admit it, but life was good. My Christmas 2006 letter was easy to write that year and longer than usual.

I had to share my wonderful experience on Whidbey Island and the fact that my book was finally being written. I was amazed that I learned to tap into the memory of the little girl I was in the 40's. With a little help she can supply everything I need to write her story.

I told them about losing Gizmo, my little shitzu dog. He developed serious heart problems and had to be put to sleep. It left such a hole in my heart and my life, I went on line to find another fur baby friend. Shitzus are so sweet, I decided to find another one. Gizmo was black and white and I couldn't have one that looked like him. I found a sweet little champagne colored lady named Pumpkin. She is just what I needed. She's only eighteen months old, so still romps and plays like a puppy.

She has quickly filled that empty place in my heart and charms everyone she meets. I want to take her to hospitals as a therapy dog. She's perfect. She's beautiful, loves everyone, loves to wear doggy clothes and does adorable tricks.

Mary Ellen and Jeff, will be in their new home sometime this year. That means I will be busy turning this house into my home for the rest of my life. All my things have been in storage so long I don't even know what I have. I'm really looking forward to starting over.

I'm looking forward to another trip to Whidbey Island too. We are having a reunion in June. I'm hoping to have my book ready to fine-tune.

I have learned so much since selling the house. I used to cry when I passed it. Now I know it's just one of those "things" we think are so important. Life is what is really precious. It's also short. I plan to use the rest of mine as wisely as I can.

Life BEGINS AT SEVENTY FIVE

Chapter Ten

Is anyone out there?

I started 2007 determined to get the book ready to polish during my trip to Whidbey Island. My expectations for that trip were exhilarating.

I must admit I wasn't enjoying being alone. I realize I am a person who needs to be part of a couple. I need someone to care for and someone who cares for me. I knew at my age I would probably be alone for the rest of my life but that doesn't mean I shouldn't meet new people and socialize. To that end, I joined one of the internet dating services. Most of my contacts lived so far away, they could only be pen pals. Even that wasn't bad. At least I had someone else to think about and talk to. I met a professor in a community college in Missouri. We wrote for several months until we had nothing new to say and the interest faded away. Then I met and dated a local man who could not be counted on. He would ask if I would like to do something that sounded great - then he just disappeared until the event was over. He must have been dating someone else and just used me to fill in the gaps.

I met one of my on line friends at a restaurant. We talked for several hours. Then he said I lived too far away. He wanted someone close enough he could call if he needed help. That old fart wasn't looking for a friend, he wanted a caregiver!

One service matched me with a man from Columbus. I refused to put a picture on line. If I wrote to someone long enough I eventually sent a picture. He said he didn't want to meet me because I had no picture. I sent word that I didn't understand his problem. I saw his picture and I was willing to meet him anyway!

I've given up on the internet
scene. Lonely is better than feeling
like a fool.

I took Pumpkin to obedience school.
I wanted to get her certified as a
therapy dog. They used a silly clicker
to give commands and I just could not
deal with it. I guess the dog is
trainable but I am not. So much for
that idea. She's definitely my therapy
dog and the cutest animal I've ever
owned.

The trip to Whidbey Island in June
was everything I dreamed it would be.
Seeing all my writing friends again was

wonderful. Angie had written her book which I eagerly read. I still think it should be a movie. It just hasn't been discovered. Mindi and I got more acquainted, arriving at the same time at the airport and taking the same ferry to the island. She has such a talent to draw you into whatever she is writing about. You live it with her. Sukie had us all gasping at her erotic essay about her midnight shower at marsh house. What a fantastic group!

Mindi and I left the island together. It was such a dramatic feeling, standing on the back of the ferry, watching the island fade into the distance as we moved into our futures. I was excited about my book but could never have dreamed of where life would lead me next.

Back in Kentucky, I worked on the book but was interrupted by the notice of our fifty-fifth class reunion in Galion. Our class had remained close. We have a luncheon twice a year for anyone who can make it. We've had our five year reunions and several mini reunions.

In early September I received a phone call from a classmate, Paul, in Cincinnati. He had broken his foot and was unable to drive. Someone in Galion told him I was coming from Kentucky and suggested that he call me. I told him I would be glad to drive him to the reunion.

A few days before the trip, he called that he had developed a blood clot and would be in the hospital.

At the reunion I had the class sign a get well card for him and gathered up the souvenirs he would have taken home. I asked him if he would like to drive with me to the luncheon in October. He said he would like that, so we stayed in touch by phone until the trip to Galion.

Paul and I grew up about three blocks apart but we ran with different groups of friends. He attended the South Elementary school and I went to the West School. I only recall seeing him once in front of the area grocer where we went to buy penny candy. We must have been seven or eight at the time. He asked to play ball with us on the depot grounds. One of the more out spoken girls in our group said, "No". I had no idea why and I didn't question. I was such a poor player, I may have feared she would send me away if I took issue with her.

All Galion students in that era went to the same Junior High which was on the second floor of the West Elementary building. The High School was two blocks up the street. Again, we ran in different groups. I only remember seeing him in the marching band at the ball games. We did not have any classes together so I knew very little about him.

He had married and was living in Cincinnati. He and his wife came to our house trying to interest us in selling Amway. We weren't interested and didn't see them again. She also died of cancer the year after I lost Les.

My book was finally finished and I
could tell my classmates about it.
Getting it published was my next
challenge and that is a big one. I will
be published. I have promised myself
that. It may take a lot of prayer,
along with a lot of hard work and being
just plain pushy…..but I can do that! I
know what I have written is something I
had to say and something that should be
read by others. I can do this!

Mary Ellen and her husband Jeff are
still hard at work on the log cabin. We
thought it would take about a year for
them to get it far enough along to live
in. We were a little off. We've had

our third Christmas together. Actually,
that's not a bad thing. We get along
well. This is a happy home. We are
definitely crowded with people and
stuff...but also with laughter and love.
The cabin will be ready when the cabin
is ready and we will be happy together
until then- Whenever "then" is.

Meanwhile, life is good. My count
on great grandbabies is now 14. Not bad
for an only child! I also managed to go
to Florida to visit my sister-in-law and
my daughter Cindy. Hopefully I can make
it to Alabama this year. I have a
sister-in-law, stepson and several

nieces there I haven't seen in many
years.

LIFE BEGINS AT SEVENTY FIVE

Chapter eleven

Getting Acquainted

After the Galion trip, Paul insisted on taking me out for dinner as a thank you. That led to more dinners and movies. He still couldn't drive so I drove to his house for our "dates". It wasn't long before I was spending as much time at Paul's as I was at home. I'm sure my daughter was plotting when she told me Pumpkin was a problem for them when I was gone and I should take her with me. That extended date time to entire weekends.

Conversation was easy for us. We shared so many experiences and had developed typical small town ideas about how things should be, plus we both loved "big band" music and crossword puzzles. Most of our "dates" were spent sitting at the kitchen table working crossword puzzles and listening to our favorite big bands.

I don't know if it was simply providence or some meddling was involved. When Paul and I became engaged, my son-in-law tore an entire wall out of the double wide to repair water damage. It was the section in the dining area and my bedroom. The work

took much longer than they thought it
would and they asked me to stay at
Paul's until the repair was finished.

Then they decided Jeff needed the
space in the storage building, so my
piano and doll collection was moved to
Paul's house along with my computer.
Looking back on it, it really sounds
like a conspiracy. What ever the motives
were, it all worked out well. After our
engagement I stayed with Paul.

My Piano was placed in the
basement. The room was semi finished
with painted walls and carpet on the
floor. I looked on line for a piano

teacher and found one less than 30 minutes away.

The reason I didn't learn more when I took lessons as a child was the teachers insisted I play only classics. All I really wanted from the piano was to learn to play the popular songs I loved to sing so I could accompany myself. I wasn't pleased playing the classics and I practiced very little. My new teacher said I could play anything I wanted to learn as long as it was within my skill level. We started with popular songs I had sung in the past and Bach. Bach is my favorite classical composer. I still don't practice enough but I am learning in spite of myself.

Now that my book is finished, I'm searching for a publisher. I had received many rejection letters over the years from my short stories and children's books. I was sure at seventy five I could not live long enough to find a traditional publisher. That meant paying a print on demand publisher to print my book. I spent hours going over requirements and offers from various publishers and finally decided on one. There was a lot of bad press on them but that was true of all of them. As it turned out, the book was beautiful and the services included were fair and reasonable.

After all those years, it was such a thrill to hold that book in my hands. It was not as awesome as giving birth but it certainly had some of those qualities about it. Now, would anyone read it? It was my story about my childhood in a small town at war. It was my story and my words about my town and my country.

When I received the galley copy of Everyone's Child, I took it to a church luncheon to brag about it. It was passed around the table for everyone to

admire. Someone asked what I planned to
write next. I said I had a children's
book I had written some time ago but
didn't have someone to illustrate it for
me. I heard a cough from the back of
the room, obviously meant to attract
attention. I wasn't aware that Debbi
Kern, one of the women in the group was
a retired art teacher. She loved
drawing animals and agreed to look at
the book. We worked together on it and
a great partnership has grown from that
beginning.

I wanted to introduce my book in my
home town, Galion, Ohio. Some of my
classmates introduced me to the local

historical society. They agreed to let me hold a book signing at the church hall across from Brownella Cottage. The cottage had been the home of the Episcopal Bishop Brown. There were covered walkways from the cottage (a very big imposing structure) to the garages and out buildings that sprawled to the next block. As children we heard and told stories of strange lights and shadows in those halls at night.

Presenting my book to my home town in that historical church was a special thrill too. Some of my classmates even served coffee and delicious home made cookies to the people who came to hear my presentation.

A store in Galion agreed to carry my book. Susan at The Evergreen Company is a friend and carries all my books.

From the time I was a little girl I wanted to be a writer but I was never sure anyone would enjoy what I would write. I feel validated knowing there are people who enjoy by book. Life just can't be any better or can it? I was really beginning to think of myself as a writer and life was so much easier sharing it with Paul. We had both made it clear marriage was not in our future.

Then one morning, at the breakfast table, Paul said, "We ought to get married." I gulped as he simply changed the subject without even taking a breath.

"No," I shouted. "You can't say something like that and just change the subject!" That day was spent discussing the possibility of a marriage. I couldn't keep it to myself. I told Mary Ellen I was planning a wedding. I still have the email she sent. It still brings a tear.

Mom,

I just wanted to let you know that I smile and occasionally shed happy tears every time I think about you and Paul getting married. Everything you have been through in your life makes this so special. I just

can't find the words to express how much
joy I feel for both of you. Life is so
tough sometimes and then….Something touches
you so deeply to make you feel just happy
to be alive.

Thanks and congratulations!!!

Paul and I thought we had all the

planning under control. We would be

married in my church. My friend and

priest, Heather, would marry us. It

would be an afternoon wedding with just

our children and grandchildren with us.

Mary Ellen jumped in and said we

had to have a reception. She took over.

We had originally decided on the first

Saturday in November. A big event that

included many of my family members was

already planned so we changed to the

second Saturday. That turned out to be the first day of deer hunting season. We quickly discovered half the state of Kentucky was opposed to that plan. The third Saturday found every suitable hall already in use. Finally the 28th met all our needs.

Mary Ellen wanted to have the reception at the two hundred year old cabin they have been working on for so long. It is still a work in progress but complete enough they are living there. It has been a labor of love and it shows. It's a warm inviting home with a glorious history and just enough

modern touches to make it comfortable
and beautiful.

Paul had been fighting off a cold
for over a week. His son and best man,
Keith, planned an evening out for his
dad, but Paul was too sick to go. Mary
Ellen and Jeff insisted I stay with them
at the cabin until the wedding.

The big day finally arrived, and
what a day it was! The sun was shining
on an almost balmy day. Paul was feeling
a little better and everything was
coming together. Just one little
problem. The cold caught up with me and
settled in my throat. I couldn't say a

word. I couldn't even cough out loud.
I think it was a beautiful wedding. I
remember bits of it through my fever.

Mary Ellen was my Maid of Honor. I
couldn't have managed that day without
her. She helped me dress and put on my
makeup. Paul and I both moved through
the day in a feverish haze. Words are
such a big part of my life. Words,
words, words and I was unable to speak
any of them.

Our kids put together a fabulous
reception. The hall was beautiful and
the food was delicious. My memories are
a bit hazy but they are beautiful.

Life just can't be any better - or can it?

Somehow, we got through the day. My taste buds were well enough to know the food was delicious. My daughter-in-law Cecilia outdid herself on the cake. It was absolutely gorgeous and tasted as good as it looked.

Looking about the reception hall was a joy, seeing our families getting to know each other and laughing together. I may only remember it in bits and pieces, but I will always cherish every moment of that day. It proves what I have been saying. Life

begins at seventy five! We are so happy

and looking forward to our life

together.

LIFE BEGINS AT SEVENTY FIVE

Chapter Twelve

Four Times!

I always enjoyed seeing older couples walking hand in hand and resented the fact that life had somehow denied me the joy of a life long relationship. My first marriage ended in divorce but he is deceased, as are my second and third husbands. Outliving three men is a little unusual but marrying a fourth is really a conversation starter. Paul went with me for an appointment with a new Doctor. When the Doctor discovered I had been widowed three times he excused himself.

I found out later, he went to Paul and said, "You know, you are number four and they are all dead! She's in my office and can't go anywhere. Run!"
It's one of our favorite stories to tell.

With the history we share, settling into married life has been easy. We still listen to big band music, but our love for crosswords seems to have faded. We've gotten very good at just relaxing and enjoying the music.

In every earlier marriage, we lived in my home. Moving into what felt like another woman's home was a little uncomfortable. No one made me feel that way. It's just how I am.

I have remained close to each family I have married into and plan to simply enlarge my family with Paul's family. That's why I love being called Grandma Nancy. Most of the grandchildren have a grandma with the same last name they have. This way I'm never in competition with another Grandma. I want them to know and love that Grandma too.

The first real change I made was in the yard. I had a beautiful yard at "everyone's house". I convinced Paul we could have a beautiful front yard. We dug up the triangle of land between the drive and sidewalk that led to the front porch. I filled it with roses, Russian sage, coreopsis and bright perennials that could be picked. By the end of the first season, cars actually stopped to complement the bright beautiful garden. Paul, always graciously told them his wife planned it and allowed him to water it!

I keep saying life can't get any better but somehow it does! There have been so many dark corners in my life and now there isn't a shadow in sight! Paul and I have completed a beautiful year of marriage filled with love and accomplishment. We've had life's trials too - Paul's blood clot in his lung and eye surgery that was less than successful were a challenge but we have been blessed. His health is improving and his eyesight is in tact. My stroke scare was just that - a scare and an opportunity to take better care of myself.

My children's book, A Garden! A Garden! came out in July and is doing very well. Debbi, my friend and illustrator has been contacted by another author to illustrate her book. I know she will become well known as an illustrator. Her talent just can't be ignored. The two of us are trying to become well known too. We are working on the next in the series with the moon and the turtle guiding the reader to new animal stories.

I always thought the act of writing was the hard part of being a writer. It's the easy part! Marketing and promotion is the real challenge. It's a constant struggle to get my work recognized. Some people manage to get their work in front of the right editor at the right moment and they get published. It's a little like winning the lottery. The odds of it happening are about the same. You get frustrated

submitting, pay a print on demand
publisher, and find book stores refuse
to carry self published books. It's
really frustrating, but doing readings
and signings and meeting adorable kids
and parents who love my book makes it
all worth while.

If this isn't enough excitement,
Paul and I are going to Italy in April!
We are so excited about the things we
will see - Rome, the Sistine Chapel, and
Michelangelo's David. We'll walk in the
ruins of Pompeii and the beaches of
southern Italy. Then the most exciting
part - 6 days in Sicily. I'm going to
see all the things Daddy told me about

when I was a little girl. I'm going to
follow his memories and do something he
never was able to do. He wanted to look
into Mt. Etna but he was a little boy
and wasn't allowed to go up the
mountain. I have Daddy's eyes and they
are going to look into the volcano for
him.

Life BEGINS AT SEVENTY FIVE

Chapter 13

That trip!

The thought of going to Italy was so exciting, I think I started packing on New Year's Day! Actually I was only planning our wardrobes. It was a 16 day tour so we would have to plan very carefully to travel light and have enough clothes. I haunted the sales racks for pretty pants suits in polyester fabric. They wouldn't wrinkle and would take up very little space. We found dark slacks for Paul in good fabric so he could wear them multiple times. Light weight wrinkle free shirts made his packing easier. We decided we could make it with each of us taking a maximum size carry on and checking just one large suitcase.

Mary Ellen and Jeff would keep Pumpkin. That made going easier for me. I knew she would be happy and well cared for while I was gone. She had lived with all of us in the double wide so she considered them family too.

My writing was taking a back seat temporarily. I was working on a follow up to A Garden! A Garden! It just wasn't as pressing as writing had been in the past.

We would not leave for Italy until April 23, 2011 but that trip was every moment of our lives from January 1. We made lists of the things we would pack in each suitcase. We notified the neighbors so they would keep an eye on the house while we were gone and Keith, Paul's son would stop a few times to be sure everything was ok.

We arranged to stop the mail and the paper. Each day something was crossed off the "to do" list and each day I got more excited than the day before. I had dreamed of one day going to Italy but in my very wildest dreams never thought it was a possibility.

The time drew near and Mary Ellen
asked us to stay at the cabin the night
before our flight to Washington DC. We
would fly from there to Rome. Mary
Ellen said they would take us to the
airport so we didn't have to pay for
long term parking. They would pick us
up when we returned and our car would be
there for us to drive home. She can
always see the best way to do things and
is always there for me when I need her.

The long awaited day arrived. I
said goodbye to my precious fur baby. I
knew Pumpkin would have the best of care
and probably wouldn't even miss me.
That didn't work two ways. I knew she

would be on my mind often. We pulled up to the airport, said goodbye and headed for the counter to check our big bag. Security went by quickly and we headed for the train and the bus ride to our flight terminal.

The flight to Washington was uneventful. Dulles International is a huge airport but it is all a blur in my memory. My family told me they would expect beautiful descriptions of everything we saw and how we felt when we saw it. I had taken a briefcase with everything I would need to keep a record as we traveled.

I wrote my first entry as we took off for Rome...................*Paul and I were simply former classmates such a short time ago. Now we sit side by side on a Triple 7 jet plane on our way to the trip of a lifetime and to complete my pilgrimage to find Daddy's home and look into Mt. Etna for him.*

The flight was an 8 hour flight. Several hours into the flight we realized old legs do not do long flights well. Our misery was made worse by a three or four year old just behind us. His mother had a small baby in her arms so his daddy was in charge of him. He had obviously never been told "no". He wasn't at all satisfied with Daddy being

his caregiver and was very vocal about

his feelings. That child didn't cry, he

screamed, all the way to Rome- one

shrill scream after another. I told the

man beside me as we took off the child

would probably go to sleep when we got

in the air. I was very wrong. He

screamed the entire trip. I turned my

music up loud in my earphones but

couldn't escape the noise. I really

wanted to talk to those parents. They

had no parenting skills at all. Like so

many young parents they never challenge

the child so he can understand he will

not always get his way in this world.

I'm sure they were embarrassed by his

behavior but they need to understand they caused it. When children are disciplined and learn to behave in public, trips are so much more enjoyable for the parents and the children, - not to mention the people around them. Parents have to understand babies are perfect little creatures when they arrive. They only become monsters if the parents fail to help them learn about the world they will have to live in and the rules they will have to follow to get along with others.

LIFE BEGINS AT SEVENTY FIVE

Chapter Fourteen

The Tour

We arrived in Rome at 8:30 AM local time. We met a rep from the tour company. He guided us to a place where we would meet our tour director who would take us to our bus. Daniella, our director, was a very attractive Sicilian woman with a slight raspy voice and a beautiful accent. It was soon evident how lucky we were to have this woman to direct us. She would lead us and worry over us like a mother hen. She took eighteen very different people from all around the globe and shaped us into a

loving family. We were equally blessed
that Giuseppe was our driver. His
driving skills were phenomenal. We soon
lost our fears of the sharp curves and
turns in the Italian landscape. We were
safe with Giuseppe.

Paul and I watched the traffic in
absolute awe. Most of the cars were
smart cars. They were parked in every
way imaginable . . . .and unimaginable!
Daniella told us they don't get excited
about scratches and dents. There is no
point in fixing them. They will just
happen again.

Our hotel was on a street too narrow for the bus. We parked on a main street and followed Daniella several blocks. She gave everyone keys and told us to meet in the lobby at four.

I had read that Hotels in Europe are not nice at all by our standards so I was pleasantly surprised. The room itself was very nice with one very big exception. It was furnished with three beds - really cots about 18 inches off the floor with really hard mats for mattresses. We were so tired even those horrible mats were welcome. We napped until meeting time.

The meeting was really to get to know one another. None of us could have imagined how close we would become or how much we would know about one another.

Our first day in Rome was Easter Monday. In Italy, Easter Monday is a holiday. We took in the sites that were open. We would see the Sistine Chapel at 7:15 Tuesday AM and the Vatican after that.

We took a whirlwind tour of Rome. We saw the coliseum, the remains of the wall around Rome, and the forum. We covered history from 200 BC to the

1800's. We saw the aqueducts and many of the famous ruins in Rome.

We went back to the hotel to shower and dress for a special welcoming meal at a popular roman restaurant. How special it was! Antipasto followed by pasta followed by pork and vegetables followed by gelato with berries and coffee. All served with an endless supply of white and red wine, guitar and clarinet music and served by a waiter with a glorious voice. It was a meal and a night to remember forever.

The next morning we were at the Sistine Chapel for our 7:15 appointment.

We met our local Guide Alexandro. He was a tall handsome Italian who was a walking encyclopedia. I wish I could remember a tenth of what he told us.

As it turned out the Vatican was being prepared for the beatification of Pope John Paul II the next week. The crowds were very heavy but being with the tour got us into every thing with minimum waits. The Pieta in St Peters was so beautiful. I thought nothing could be more beautiful but that was before I saw Michelangelo's David. We were able to go through the catacombs before we left Rome. What a city of endless history.

in Florence we stayed at the
Michelangelo Hotel. What a difference.
Our room was small but very nice. The
bed was not great but much better than
the cot in Rome.

We are getting to know our
traveling partners. As in all groups
there are people you really enjoy and
some you'd rather not know too well. Our
group was a lot of fun, even the two
sisters who can't seem to get anywhere
on time. They really get along like
sisters — always putting one another
down! Still, they are friendly well
meaning people. There are two couples
who have been so good to us. They know

we are probably too old for the activity of this tour. We took the tour because it said moderate physical activity. That might be true for 40 year olds. But we are 77 and this is not moderate. They have been such great help, carrying our bags when the trip is long or up hill. They are from Australia and New Zealand. I hope to stay in touch with them and maybe lure them to America to visit us.

Today we saw Michelangelo's David. What a thrill. He is so perfect you feel like you can see his muscles flex. I had to buy photos because our pictures didn't come out or maybe we accidentally wiped them out. We just got the camera and neither of us does well with new electronics.

We ate on the square in Florence. It was the best meal yet…..maybe. The food here is so good, your best meal is the one you are eating now!

We returned to our room. The hardest part of tours is the wake up hour. You have to have your bags packed and outside your door - usually by 6AM. You eat breakfast and climb on the bus for your next destination. It is really an exhausting pace. I am so glad we did

this now. Another year could mean we
would not be able to handle it.

After Florence we headed for
Venice. Giuseppe took us to a ferry
boat that would take us to our island
hotel.

What a welcome! We were enjoying
the salt air when we heard the siren.
Suddenly, there it was- uniformed
firemen in yellow hats with hoses on a
fire boat - everything but a truck!

Our hotel was a jewel. Several
centuries before, the venetians had
removed all the houses on one island.

They planted trees and created a green space for everyone to enjoy the outdoors for picnics. We walked through what was now a mature woods to our hotel. We took a 20 minute ferry ride from the island to Venice. Venice was our favorite city. We fell in love with the charming houses lining the canals and the beautiful buildings and churches.

A number of us gathered to ride a gondola. Our group needed two gondolas. Five women rode in one with an accordionist and an elderly singer. Our gondola with three couples stayed right behind them. If we knew the words to the songs they played we sang along. The women had turned a sharp corner so we could not see them for a few minutes. We heard a scraping sound and laughter. As we turned the corner we could see the gondolier in the first gondola. He was looking at our gondolier and laughing so hard he had tears in his eyes. I am sure his pants were not dry.

When we turned the corner enough to see the full gondola, the little man was nowhere in sight. We were all laughing and looking for him when he suddenly popped up from where he had fallen and started singing like nothing had happened.

Our last day in Venice we took a boat to the island of Burano. The women of the island took up lace making while the men were out fishing. The shops are filled with gorgeous lace goods. Our meal on Burano was definitely a seafood feast.

Leaving Venice was really sad. We would have really enjoyed more time there. We took the ferry back to the main land.

Giuseppe and our bus were waiting for us at the terminal on the main land. We are off to Assisi.

My first view of this mountaintop city was breathtaking. The bus could only take us as far as the roads can accommodate a bus. We had to walk a good distance to our hotel. Again our friends took our bags and stayed with us until we checked in to our hotel.

The hotel had once been a noble residence. In 1899 it became an 83 room hotel. Everything is special about it. Our room was beautiful and had a small iron balcony over looking a large outdoor terrace. Paul was enthralled with the beautiful nude statues that surrounded the terrace below. I was enthralled with the view from the

balcony. It was breathtaking and so
peaceful. Everything about Assisi is
spiritual. It was like discovering a
bit of heaven. We were too tired to
walk up the hill to the church and the
business area. Even without activity or
site seeing, I could have stayed there
for a very long time and been perfectly
content. I have never felt that way
about any other place. Venice and
Assisi will always be my favorite cities
in Italy. I would love to see them again
but I know I will never again take a
long flight.

Saying goodbye to Assisi was even
harder than leaving Venice, but the

thought of seeing Pompeii allowed me to
climb on the bus anticipating a
wonderful day.

It would have been very special but
it rained the entire time we were there.
We wore our raincoats and hid under
umbrellas but still could not stay dry.
I had always been fascinated by Pompeii
and read everything I could find about
it. Nothing I had read or watched
matched the thrill of actually seeing
the ruins and the bodies of those poor
souls trapped in a time capsule of one
day in history.

Our next stop was Naples. I was really getting excited now. We were just hours away from Sicily! Everyone in our group knew how important this part of the tour was to me. I had been very vocal about finding Daddy's home and seeing that volcano for him.

In Naples we boarded the boat that would deliver us to Palermo in the morning. We had a tiny room with bunk beds and a really tiny bathroom. I slept very little that night. The excitement was just too much.

In the morning I was in Daddy's Sicily at last.

LIFE BEGINS AT SEVENTY FIVE

Chapter 15

Sicily

I knew Daddy had sailed for America from Palermo. When I stepped off the boat and saw the port I couldn't hold back the tears. I could imagine a frightened little seven year old boy sailing to an unknown America. He had just said goodbye to a Grandma he adored and knew he would never see again. I am sure no one asked about or understood the pain he was feeling.

We toured the palace and the chapel. I have seen so much gold and glitter it has begun to look gaudy. I really don't care if I never see another cathedral. They are truly remarkable but seeing the grandeur on the inside in contrast to the pathetic beggars outside makes me very uncomfortable.

Lunch that day was fantastic and so unexpected. We stopped at what appeared to be a stretch of beach on the Mediterranean. We walked down wooden steps to the beautiful turquoise water. Several took of their shoes and waded into the water. We went into a wooden building with plastic wrapped around it to protect it from the wind. We found a buffet with everything simple and wonderful. There were really ripe tomatoes, mushrooms, all kinds of cheeses, tuna, sardines and the world's best olives. I tore into the ripe tomatoes. Everyone was delighted and stuffed. After all the rich food we had been eating, this simple delicious fare was just what we needed.

Our next stop was The Valley of the temples. I was so exhausted I was not impressed. Every temple looks much like the last one you saw and the one you will see next. They are all placed on hilltops that have to be climbed. I was anxious to reach our stop for the night. We had planned to have a drink before we left for dinner on a Sicilian farm. I was so tired I couldn't think of drink or food. I was so cold and had no strength at all. Daniella wanted me to see a doctor. I just wanted to rest. She wanted Paul to go to the dinner but he wouldn't leave me.

The next morning we drove to Taormina. Our room was beautiful. I could even see Mt. Etna from the corner of our balcony. I hoped being close to my goal of going to Bronte would perk me up.

I really didn't feel up to it but the trip to Mt. Etna was part of my reason for this tour. We were guided by

another small Sicilian woman with an
even raspier voice than Daniella. She
told us we would go as close to the top
as tourist are allowed. Mt. Etna is the
most active volcano in Europe and too
dangerous to allow anyone near the top.
I wanted to look into that mountain for
Daddy. I did see fissures of old
eruptions and our final stop was a
blackened area that was the crater of a
previous eruption. The landscape was
beautiful until we reached this charred
area. I told the guide I was going to
Bronte. She told me the scenery on that
side of the mountain would be smoke
stained and dark. My expectations for

Bronte were so filled with hope I couldn't imagine a dark dreary place.

When we returned to our hotel we called home to see how everyone was and to check on my dog, Pumpkin. My daughter said my granddaughter wanted to reach me. She tried to find some of the places my father had talked about and in the process she found a cousin we didn't know existed. He wanted me to call him when I arrived.

Daniella found us a driver we could hire to take us to Bronte. I called my cousin, Luigi, to tell him we would be in Bronte for a few hours and our driver would take us back to the hotel. Luigi said the family wanted to meet me and planned a dinner for us that evening. Our driver should drop us off and Luigi would take us back to the hotel after dinner.

Driving to Bronte that afternoon was fascinating. Our driver, Salvatore, gave us the history of each area and village we passed through. It seemed so right to go to Bronte with Salvatore. That was my grandfather's name.

When we arrived in Bronte I was pleased that it was not as dark and dreary as the guide at Mt. Etna described it. We called Luigi from a little square with a fountain. We paid our driver and in minutes we were meeting Luigi's mother, father and sister. It was like visiting my relatives when I was a child. I felt like I had known these people all my life.

I showed them the picture of Daddy's house. They knew exactly where it was. I still can't believe that day. Luigi drove us to the house and we proceeded to take pictures in front of it. We attracted so much attention people were on their balconies and on the street, asking what we were doing.

A young man came from the house next
door. I told him my grandfather built
the house and my father was born there.
He said his family had just bought the
house and offered to let us go inside.
The tears could not be held back. I felt
truly blessed. I have pictures sitting
in the house Daddy left in 1913.

Bronte is a large producer of
pistachios. Luigi took us to a shop to
enjoy pistachio gelato. It was
delicious as was the wonderful meal the
family prepared for us. We had
spaghetti with delicious local sausage.
The other sisters and husbands came in
to meet us. We speak no Italian and

they speak no English. Luigi, fortunately speaks perfect English. He was our interpreter. It was a wonderful time with my new family. No memory is more beautiful to me than sitting at that table filled with food and love in Bronte.

That evening we said goodbye to my new family. I understand a little of how daddy felt saying goodbye to people he loved, knowing he would never see them again. Luigi said he would try to come to America for a visit. I am waiting.

Luigi and his brother-in-law drove us back to Taormina. I worried about them driving so late. It was 11:30 when they dropped us off at our hotel.

I slept well in spite of the adrenalin pumping through my body. The next morning at breakfast our friends told us when Daniella told them we were not at dinner because we were on our way to Bronte - everyone cheered. Our tour family knew how important Bronte was to me.

After breakfast we boarded our bus for the 300 mile trip to Sorrento. After my day in Bronte everything was anti climax but none the less wonderful. It's just that I'm tired, my heart is full, my eyes are on overload and I am ready to go home.

LIFE BEGINS AT SEVENTY FIVE

Chapter 16

Journey on!

We arrived at our hotel in Sorrento in time to change for dinner. We were told this restaurant was really special. What an understatement!

A small bus took us to the area of the restaurant. We still walked several blocks through very narrow streets and alleys. Nothing looked special when we entered the building, until we came to the stairs. We walked up 3 flights of wide steps through gorgeous flowers and exotic trees. At the top we were in a huge dining room with a garden room behind it.

Our waiter was part entertainer. He ran to Paul and kissed his bald head. He called him a "bigga baby". The food was outstanding. By this point I was too tired to be hungry. I just tasted everything on my plate. I was broken hearted when I couldn't eat my desert- two cream puffs bathed in chocolate!

Our room was nice with a balcony but, obviously, good mattresses haven't hit Europe!

We had an early call for our trip to Capri. We met our local guide at the Jet Ferry. The 20 minute ride took us to the cable train that took us to the top of the mountain. Capri really caters to the "Rich and Famous." The shops are fantastic but expensive. The group walked to further explore the mountain. We were too tired to walk. We took the cable train back to the landing area. I found something I had wanted since we arrived in Italy. .soup! The wind was cool and the bay was beautiful so we sat at a table in the sun to enjoy the best vegetable soup I have ever had. When the group returned, I had a sunburned nose to show my folly.

That evening we walked through a garden to a hotel on the beach. We had another delicious meal watching a magnificent sunset over the bay.

In the morning Giuseppe and our big bus was there to take us back to Rome. The Amalfi Coast was magnificent. The village of Positano had shops filled with women's clothing. As in Capri, just looking was a treat.

In Rome, our room was much nicer than the first one. The mattress was

hard but not nearly as bad as the others
we had tried to sleep on. We dressed for
our farewell dinner. What a surprise!

We passed the Arena on soccer
night. All the parking places were taken
so they were parking their smart cars in
a row down the middle of the street.
There is not enough money to pay me to
drive in Italy!

At the Dinner Theater we were
entertained by four opera stars singing
various arias. Individually, the voices
were beautiful and together they were
fabulous. It's a good thing we go home

tomorrow. I'm running out of adjectives to describe this trip!

We came to see and learn. We leave with great memories and two new families - Our tour family and several friends we will stay in touch with and our Bronte Family we will always be part of. Arrivederci Roma!

In my Christmas letter that year I tried to tell everyone how exciting and wonderful that tour was and how thrilled I was to be allowed to go inside Daddy's home. You can't even pray for such an awesome event.

If we keep up this pace, Paul and I won't have time to grow old! The illustrations for the new book are almost ready and I'm writing another. I remember not having anything to write about. Now ideas bump into one another. Two happy years, married to Paul, has something to do with that!

This has been Paul's year for eye surgery. His first cataract surgery did not go well. The lens in one eye shattered giving him vision problems from all the debris in the eye. A specialist was able to repair the eye and remove the other cataract. He raised his eyebrows and repaired his droopy eyelids. Now he not only sees better - he looks younger than me. Not fair!

I don't think we will be doing more tours. I want to see the rest of the world from the deck of a cruise ship!

LIFE BEGINS AT SEVENTY FIVE

Chapter Seventeen

The last Bucket trip

That long flight from Italy left both of us too exhausted to do much of anything but watch TV and nap. We were tired but far from finished.

We had completed my "bucket trip" but Paul had a trip he had wanted to take for a long time. We started gathering information on combined cruises with land tours in Alaska. We would take a land tour followed by a cruise.

It started badly. Our Flight in a straight line from Chicago to Anchorage was changed. We would fly from Cincinnati to Houston to Anchorage. That put two 78 year old travelers in dangerously cramped seating on a seven hour flight.

We arrived in Anchorage totally exhausted with leg cramps so violent we could hardly walk.

After a night in Anchorage we were bused to the lodge at Denali. We always try to absorb the beauty of any place we visit. Denali is indeed a beautiful place and the lodge has windows all around to give great views of the surroundings.

We enjoyed the entertainment in Denali. The food wasn't the greatest but certainly nothing to complain about. Our bus tour of Denali was everything we could ask for. We really wanted to see Mt. McKinley. It creates its own climate and much of the time clouds and mist obscure it from sight. Many tourists don't get to see it. At the lodge we asked where it could be seen. Our waitress said if she was out she would be in that window. We only saw sky, not a trace of a mountain.

On the bus the driver said he was afraid the mountain would not be visible. On our third stop he said we might be pleased at our next stop.

When I stepped off the bus the tears just fell. A magnificent mountain looking like it was made of crystal glistened in the afternoon sun. It was a spiritual experience.

On a stop at a little shop with local artifacts, I tried to wear a moose antler for a picture but it was far too heavy for me to lift.

We were taken to a port where we boarded a boat to look for whales and see the glacier. Paul wanted to see the whales but none jumped from the water the way he wanted to see them. We did see seal colonies on the beaches we passed.

We then took a bus to the train station. The view from the train was fabulous. Denali stayed visible through most of the trip. We were seated in the last car on the train. The air conditioner broke down and the car became very hot. When the Air Conditioner was finally repaired, it was turned on full blast. It was blowing

directly on us. We asked to have it
turned down. The attendant said the
back of the car had to cool off before
they could turn it down. We stood menus
in the A/C slots trying to direct the
air away to no avail. By the time we
reached Whittier, I was hoarse and Paul
was shivering. I think the cruise was
nice but we were too ill to remember
much of it.

We finally flew home. Mary Ellen
drove our car and brought the dog to the
airport, to drive us home. Jeff drove
their car the take them home from our
house.

Mary Ellen knew she had to tell me she had been diagnosed with breast cancer. She said she caught it early and would be fine. I was so sick, processing this horrible news was difficult.

We were so tired when we got home we just collapsed. In the morning, Paul was unable to catch his breath. I took him to the emergency room. He had bronchitis and was admitted.

In the morning my daughter called me. From the sound of my voice she drove from Kentucky and took me to the emergency room. I also had bronchitis

and pneumonia in my left lung. The
doctors sent us home to recuperate.
They warned us it would be months before
we felt like ourselves. It took four
months to fully recuperate.

We are glad we saw Denali and the
mountain. Unfortunately, the negatives
of that trip outweigh the positives. We
know what companies we will not use in
the future.

Life BEGINS AT SEVENTY FIVE

Chapter Eighteen

Dark Places

The year started out normal enough. Mary and Dick, our friends in Lima, had their annual Christmas Party the first weekend in January. We stayed in Lima for three days before coming home. Paul had a pacemaker installed in December and getting the surgery to heal was a real project because of his factor five. They checked his Coumadin level often and adjusted the medication. He was definitely not feeling up to par.

A few days after we returned home he found fresh blood around the incision made to place the pacemaker. I drove him to the Emergency room. They felt he could return home and see his heart doctor the next day. His blood was checked even more frequently and he saw the doctor every week until the accumulated blood around the pacemaker began to be absorbed.

We never seem to be able to face one problem at a time. Heavy rains caused flooding in the basement level garage and laundry room. Constantly mopping and pushing the water to the drain was more than we could keep up

with. We called in a water proofer. A
sump pump installed in the garage solved
the problem.

The famous ides of March struck us
that year. Paul complained of a
terrible headache and his left arm was
numb. He had banged his head on the
doorframe of the car a few days before.
I thought of a concussion and took him
to Emergency. A cat scan revealed there
was bleeding in his brain. He was
transferred by ambulance to the
neurology ICU and University Hospital.

Our church has been so supportive
through all our calamities. I emailed

the women's group asking for prayers for Paul. I heard from them daily and have no idea how I could have survived the next several months without them.

I had another wonderful helper in my neighbor Valerie. She was always available to let the dog out if I had to be gone too long. She would let Pumpkin out in the fenced in back yard for a while each afternoon while I was at the hospital. No matter how dark my world has been I have always been blessed to have friends and neighbors who became my angels when I needed them most.

After a few days, a CT scan showed
no new bleeding so Paul was sent home
with an appointment to see a neurologist
the next week. At the appointment the
Doctor told Paul to stop taking his
Coumadin. I objected, reminding him
that Paul was Factor five and not taking
the blood thinner was dangerous. The
Doctor insisted he must stop the
medicine for two weeks. He insisted
that was something that must be done. I
gave in and Paul took the blood thinners
out of his pill boxes.

After only three days without blood
thinners Paul had severe chest pain and
difficulty breathing. The Emergency

Room found he had multiple blood clots in his lungs and immediately transferred him back to neurology ICU at University Hospital. There was no new bleeding but the dried blood that had accumulated in the brain began to cause horrible problems. He was unable to answer some of the simple questions they asked him each morning and at each shift change. I had to run into the hall the morning they asked his name and he was silent for a long time. He had the look of a totally confused child as he said "I don't know." His motor skills were very poor. He was not allowed out of bed at all. Paul was such a strong man. This total breakdown was heartbreaking.

After a few days he was transferred to the regular neurology area. The day after his transfer I had reached his floor and heard a call on the loud speaker that a patient was seizing. As I drew closer I could see everyone running into Paul's room. His nurse made him comfortable and told me if he had any problem to ring for her.

I stood by his bed to try to keep him calm. Suddenly a dimple in his cheek began to pulse and then he began to shake violently. I rang for the nurse and tried to hold him. Several nurses came in as the seizure stopped.

They asked questions about what had happened before and during the seizure. I was as frightened as Paul was and wasn't a good observer at all.

The group of doctors making rounds came in very soon. They agreed Paul should have a monitor to see what was going on in the brain when the seizures occur. They said the seizures were caused by pressure the dried blood put on a specific part of the brain. The blood would slowly be absorbed into the system but the damage caused by the pressure might not go away.

They quickly had him hooked up to a brain scan machine so his brain activity could be monitored.

The monitor was removed when he had no seizures for 24 hours. The very next morning, he had a seizure a few minutes after I arrived. The doctors gathered around his bed to plan his care. A woman neurologist suggested a particular drug and the others agreed. She looked at me and stated "He will not have another seizure." The drug worked. He has not had another seizure since then.

The doctors determined Paul would need extensive therapy before he could return home. I had to make two choices for rehab units to send him to. We were so fortunate. A bed was available at my first choice, the rehab unit at our local hospital. I knew that hospital gave excellent care but I was unaware how great the rehabilitation unit was. The rooms were all bright and homey with a large bathroom in each room. They follow a holistic program for healing. His grandchildren were allowed to visit him. Even our Shitzu dog spent time with him. She was so popular, she visited other patients too and was invited back.

I frequently ordered my meal from the cafeteria to be brought up with his meal to the big social room. We sat at one of the small tables along the wall of windows for our meal. It was like dining out and unlike most hospitals, the food was delicious.

Paul remained in rehab for a month. When he came home, nurses and therapists treated him at home until he able enough to be released.

While Paul slowly improved, another dark shadow was hovering over the family. Years earlier, Paul's son-in-law, Richard had suffered kidney failure. Paul's daughter Karyn, was a close enough match, she was able to donate a kidney which saved Richard. Time for a kidney transplant is usually 7 or 8 years. Further health issues and time took their toll on the function of the kidney. It was failing and Richard's health was failing with it.

In July, the family was gathered around his bed. With the soft sound of prayer in the room, Richard quietly left us.

I've held two men I loved in my arms and watched them die. It is not easy and it is not something you recover from quickly. Somehow, life had taught me acceptance when those tragedies occurred. Karyn has not learned that lesson and accepting is very difficult for her. She will move on, but it will be painfully slow for her and all who love her.

Every year, at Christmas, I regret not having the house to welcome the family home for Christmas. Even with the house it was getting more and more crowded. There is no place we can all be together as we have in the past. I miss the planning and the fun of having them all together.

I decided I would have my Family gathering at a summer picnic instead of the holiday. At least I would see them all and the picnic could be my gift to all of them. Mary Ellen had a caterer who was very inexpensive. The cost was something I could handle and all I needed extra was drinks. I decided to try it. I used the shelter Jeff had built at the log cabin. It offered plenty of room. When they received the invitations they called to let me know they were coming. The turn out was excellent and I was really excited. We had a beautiful summer day in August. The food was OK but not wonderful. Everyone seemed to enjoy getting together and I really enjoyed seeing all of them. I decided I would try to make it an annual affair.

It was such a pleasant break from the miseries that kept coming, I prayed the dark shadow was through with us.

Late in November, I got my answer. Mary Ellen was having a second surgery on her breast. They would remove more tissue leaving a wider area of healthy tissue. She was sure I didn't need to be at the hospital. Jeff would call me after the surgery.

I had gone to pick up my new glasses. Paul's cell rang. It was my son-in-law Jeff. Paul couldn't understand him and handed the phone to me. Jeff was obviously under great distress. He managed to blurt out that something had gone wrong in the operating room. Mary Ellen was in ICU on a ventilator. I told him we would drive there immediately.

That trip was the longest thirty minute trip in my life. I couldn't help remembering her tonsillectomy, many years before. I had waited so long and I knew a tonsillectomy didn't take long at all. I headed for the surgical floor. Just as the elevator door opened

her surgeon stepped out. He said "She

gave us a scare but she's fine now. Her

heart stopped for 22 minutes and we had

to put her on a heart machine. She will

be in her room soon and you can see her

there."

She had a reaction to the anectine

- a drug that keeps a patient from

moving about during surgery. The doctor

said we must be sure she never was given

anectine again. It would probably be

fatal. I couldn't help wondering if

that drug hadn't shown up again.

Jeff and some of his family were in the lobby when we arrived. He took us to her in ICU. The agony of seeing my lively, quick witted, beautiful daughter, so pale and helpless, and hearing the ventilator pumping air in and out of her lungs to keep her alive was such a shock. She had experienced pulmonary edema. Her lungs, for no apparent reason, had filled with fluid, making it impossible for her to breath. With out the ventilator she would have died from drowning.

There are so many strong ties between Mary Ellen and me. All my children are special but she is my baby.

The last one. She is the only girl I gave birth to. She was also the baby I nearly lost. I was given drugs to prevent miscarriage and spent the last few months I carried her as close to bed rest as I could be, with a three year old and a 6 year old to care for. Just the thought of how close we were to losing her that day still fills my heart with terror.

There was much pain in writing the Christmas letter that year. It had been a terrible year filled with every emotion in the book. I explained Mary Ellen's cancer and the terrifying pulmonary edema that almost took her from us. The heartbreaking loss of Richard and Paul's brain bleed and the seizures it caused all added to the horror of the year. Without the prayers of our church and the churches of friends I don't know what we would have done. We have learned just how fragile life really is and how healing prayer can be.

LIFE BEGINS AT SEVENTY FIVE

Chapter Nineteen

Can we Try Normal?

We prayed this would finally be an
uneventful year in the health
department. The only big problem in our
world was Paul's prostate problem. His
PSA kept climbing and the urologist he
used was knife happy. Every time we saw
him he talked about surgery. We finally
found another urologist. He was
concerned about the PSA and when it
climbed to 34.7 he sent Paul to a
Urology clinic with an oncologist.

They were very thorough and recommended radiation treatment given with a new robotic system that delivered the radiation directly to tiny areas shown with gold markers that were placed before the treatment.

The first check up after the treatment his PSA had dropped to 12. We were so relieved we had changed that Doctor.

The picnic we had in August of 2013 was such a treat for everyone I decided to try it again. The food the year before wasn't the greatest and new caterers were really expensive. Mary Ellen wanted to cook the burgers which we bought in large rolls to simply slice

off into burgers. I made my only claim
to fame, which is my potato salad. Ceil
took over the pasta part with her
wonderful Lasagna. We had slaw, sliced
tomatoes and all the fixings for great
hamburgers. There was plenty of tea,
lemonade and water. Anyone who wanted
something stronger or different was
welcome to bring it. A grandson found a
baker who bakes for a hobby. He made
the most delicious and well decorated
cake I have ever seen.

The shelter at the cabin was
packed. We couldn't have asked for a
nicer day. It was sunny, breezy and not
too hot. The horse shoes and corn hole

sets were kept busy. Debbi, my illustrator, who is also a great photographer, took pictures so we can enjoy that day over and over.

In September, we made our annual trip to the Smokey Mountains. We talked to the rangers in Gatlinburg and found that Elk had been released into the mountains. They usually came in around supper time at the Oconaluftee Visitors Center and Farm Museum. We drove down and sat on the porch waiting. We noticed a big crowd along the river and walked down to see what they were so excited about. A gorgeous big bull was on the other side of the river. Three

females were standing in the water close
to the edge. A park ranger came down
and told everyone to back off. The
animals wanted to get to the field to
graze but would not come out of the
water with everyone standing there.
When the crowd moved away the cows moved
up to the field and began to eat. It
really made our day watching these
beautiful creatures making themselves at
home in an area that had once been
overrun with Elk until they were hunted
to extinction.

The preservation of animals and
reintroduction of once native animals is
a successful part of the national park

system. We should all be grateful for these wonderful programs that give us a wonderful natural place to explore and enjoy.

I am also a rock hound. I love rocks. They are so unique and beautiful. I found a rock shop that has great samples of all sizes. I brought two nice specimens home last trip and plan to bring more each time we go there.

LIFE BEGINS AT SEVENTY FIVE

Chapter Twenty

Just Beginning!

Spring is really wet this year. That makes the spring garden clean up difficult. It also makes it hard for me to get into the garden. I'm never happy until I can feel the dirt under my fingernails. I think the reason I love spring so much is because it is so much like real life. No matter how dark and miserable things are, spring will come and make everything fresh and new again.

That's the way my life has been. Some of my winters have been so tough I'd think I'd never be happy again.

Then a spring would come. Someone or something gave me a new direction to follow. Every spring has been wonderful but the spring of my seventy-fifth year offered a promise like no other.

I finished the book I decided to write when I was fifteen and began to blossom as an author.

I met Debbi who shared my interest in animals, children and children's books. My words and her illustrations have built a great friendship and a viable business venture.

I fell in love again and found I would not have to walk through life alone. I have that someone to walk hand in hand with through my autumn years.

I feel as invincible as I did in my youth. I can't think of anything I can't do or accomplish. I have so many ideas for books for both adults and children. I have causes I want to write for.

I want to be part of the reason laws will be passed to really punish those who abuse and neglect animals. We know those who are capable of cruelty to animals are frequently equally capable of harming babies, the elderly or any helpless person. Yet, we give them a

tiny fine and a slap on the hand. I want
to see animal cruelty become a felony
with jail time and life long monitoring.

Paul and I will enjoy vacations and
traveling as long as we can. I think we
are ready for shorter trips, closer to
home. We will continue to go to the
Smokey Mountains every year. We both
really enjoy that time. We've seen it
so often, yet it is more beautiful and
inspiring with each visit.

Life not only begins at seventy-
five, it gets better with each passing
year. I will welcome eighty-two this
year and rejoice in all the things I can

still do. I won't dwell on what I can no longer do, but be grateful I could do them this long.

Unlike Mama, I will never be angry if I recover from a close call at deaths door. I don't fear death, but I find life an exciting gift. I treasure every day I am given and look forward to discovering every tomorrow I am blessed with.

The thrill of being able to decide what to do with another day is always rewarding. Any time I have an opportunity to do something I have never done before, I jump at the chance.

Sometimes my plate is just too full and I have to drop something. As soon as I rest a bit I find something to pile back on my plate. That may sound like a vicious circle but life is to live and I try not to waste a minute of it.

Life begins at seventy-five. What you do with that opportunity is up to you. If you are open and receptive to change, you will seize each new day, live it and enjoy it. You never know where it will lead you!

www.ingramcontent.com/pod-product-compliance
Lightning Source LLC
Chambersburg PA
CBHW031157270326
41931CB00006B/306